This book belongs to:

Are you ready to open a new window?

Can you use all the letters, from A to Z, to explain the story of *your* name?

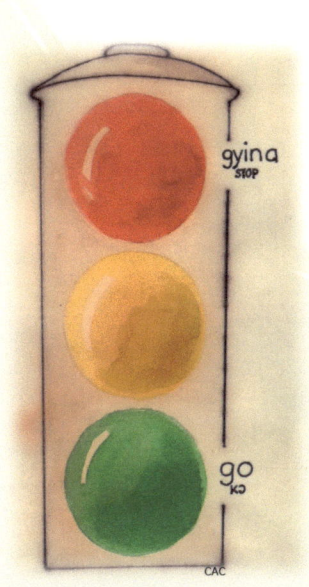

My Name is an Address
by Ekuwah [Mends] Moses
Published by EduMatch®
PO Box 150324, Alexandria, VA 22315

www.edumatch.org

© 2021 [Ekuwah Mends Moses]
All rights reserved. No portion of this book may be reproduced in any form without permission from the publisher, except as permitted by U.S. copyright law. For permissions contact:

sarah@edumatch.org

ISBN: 978-1-953852-30-4

Acknowledgements:

My Name is an Address was designed through a compilation of the professional art of Carolyn Coffield Mends **(CAC)**
and the
authentic artifact collection of Albion Mends III

Creative Assistance:
Albion Mends III and Effuah Sam

In loving memory of Carolyn Coffield Mends, my mother

A Note from Ekuwah

Akwaaba! Welcome to the ABC story of my name! Did you know that a name includes history, geography, and migration? Language, culture, and heritage are also linked to a person's name. I chose to use the letters of the alphabet to show how wide and deep names can go.

My life began in Warrensburg, Missouri, but that is not my full address. I am the second child of an immigrant and an African-American. *My Name is an Address* features my father's family line. Unfortunately, much of my mother's African ancestry is unknown. Family lines were stripped from enslaved Africans as they were involuntarily and forcibly transported all over the world. Slavery, war, trade, colonialism, and other world events changed families forever – including mine. I am proud that I can use my first and last name to trace my father's ancestors back to Ghana, West Africa. I hope to discover more information about my mother's African origin. She wholeheartedly celebrated our Ghanaian heritage and cultures of the world.

I call myself the "designer" of this book because the handwriting and drawings were painted by my remarkable mother. The illustrations are a collage of my parents' treasures. The words are my way of explaining how they fit together and shaped the person I am today.

As you read, I hope you enjoy our photographs and artifacts. I hope you feel my parents' love and guidance. I hope you learn some of our culture and traditions. I hope you read how I embrace my name and identity. I hope you gain tools for facing challenges. I hope you get inspired to research your own name. I hope you write your story before someone else shares it for you. Tell your authentic story! The world needs to hear your voice!

My Name is an Address

by
Ekuwah [Mends] Moses

EduMatch®

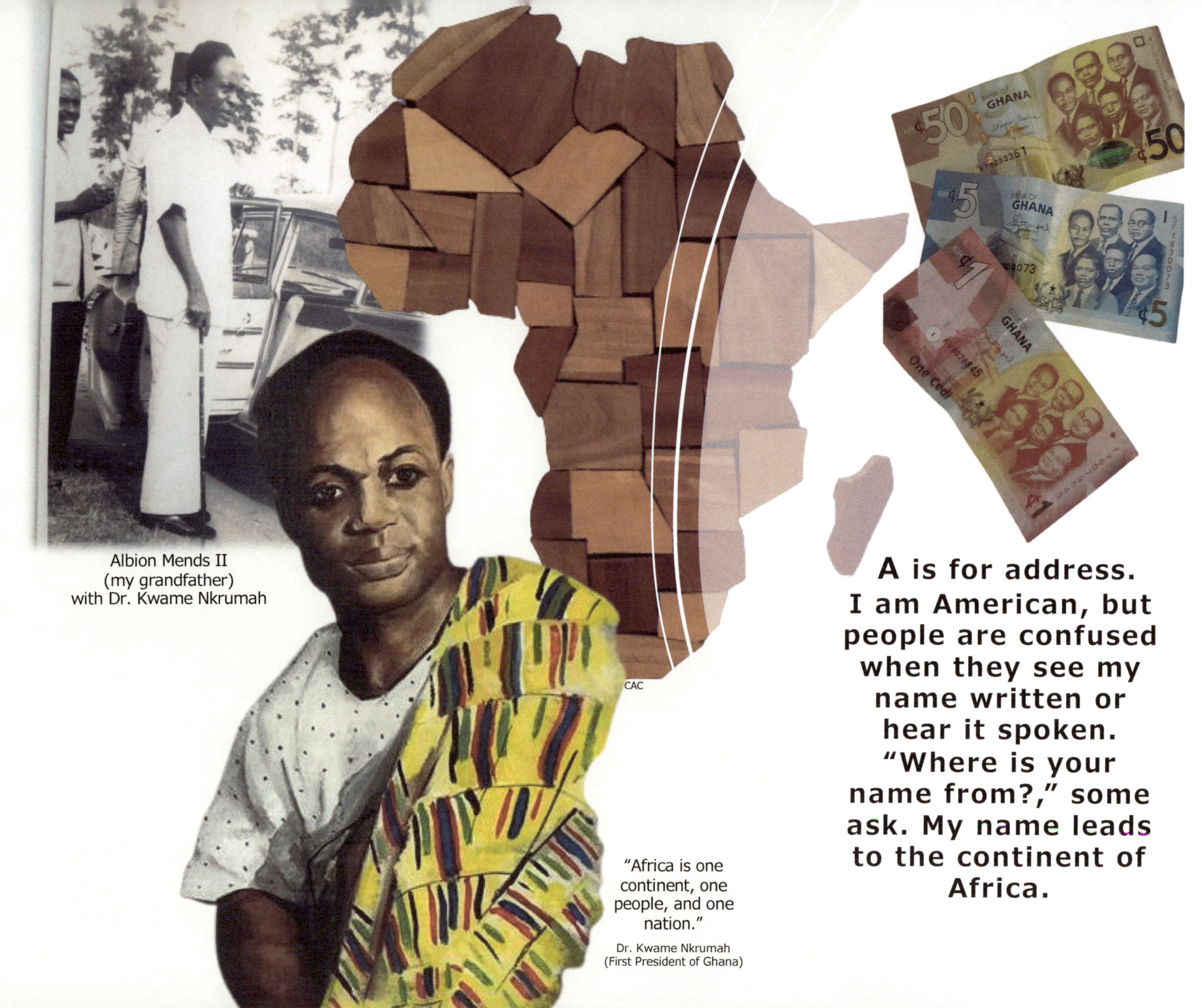

Albion Mends II (my grandfather) with Dr. Kwame Nkrumah

"Africa is one continent, one people, and one nation."

Dr. Kwame Nkrumah (First President of Ghana)

A is for address. I am American, but people are confused when they see my name written or hear it spoken. "Where is your name from?," some ask. My name leads to the continent of Africa.

B is for born.
My father was born in Cape Coast, Ghana. He lived in a two-story compound house. It is in a busy neighborhood called Kawanupadu. Our extended family still lives there. Generations of family pictures are hung high on the walls.

Albion Mends II
Georgina Isabella Sagoe
(my grandmother's family home)

1940s
B71 Canaan Lodge
Saltpond, Ghana
(a mansion built by Albion Mends I)

2020

Albion Mends I
(my great-grandfather)
Kwamina Anamuah

James Felix Mends
(my great-great-grandfather)
not pictured

Albion Mends II
(my grandfather)

Albion Mends III
(my father)
Papa Kojo Anamuah

C is for change. Some coastal Ghanaians were baptized and renamed when enrolled in the British education system. Albion means "old England." Mends may be linked to a British Royal Navy admiral who patrolled the Gold Coast. Our family's indigenous name is Anamuah. We choose to keep the Mends surname because it can be traced back to our family. There are people with the same last name in the cities of Cape Coast, Ada, and Saltpond. Mends is my maiden name.

with PAPA

and MAMA

D is for distinct. Mama and Papa gave me a name that is distinct from the names of most people. I am thankful they decided to follow a cultural tradition. It is a name that is common in Papa's country.

Ekuwah writes her name.

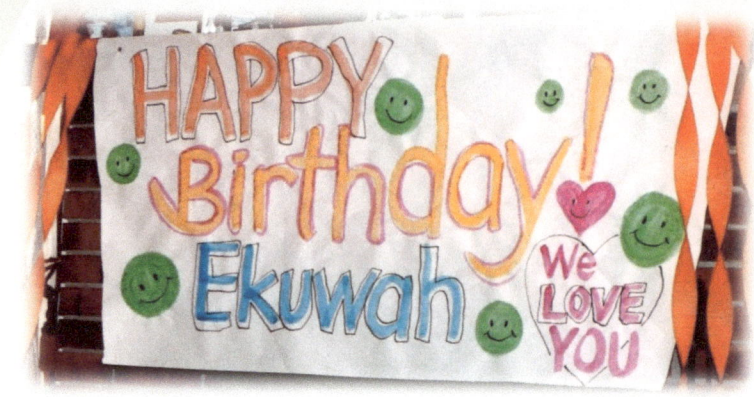

E is for examples.
Ekuwah is my first name and leads to my ancestors' country. My middle name, Ruth, leads to my Christian religion. I have cousins with the same first name, but their parents chose a more traditional Fante spelling – Ekua. My grandfather suggested the spelling of my name.

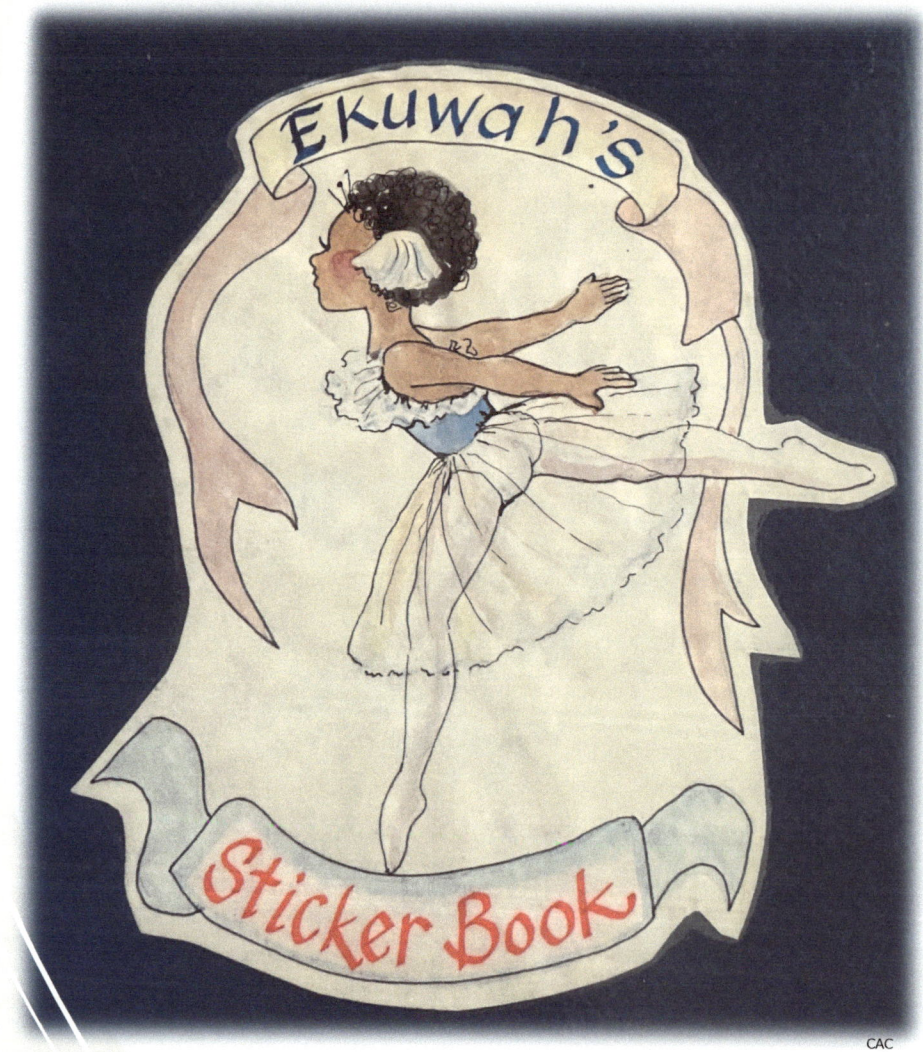

F is for facts.
I am Fante. Fante people mainly live along the coastal regions of Ghana. Tourists visit the forts and dungeons to see where the Dutch, Portuguese, and British colonizers kept enslaved people. They want to learn how Africans were captured, tortured, and exported. They wonder how their families were impacted by the slave trade. They want to discover if their roots lead to Ghana.

NANA'S YARD IN GHANA

Cape Coast
1981

Cape Coast Slave Dungeon
"Door of Return"
July 2013

shackles used on enslaved people

G is for gold.
Ghana is in West Africa. It was called the Gold Coast until the end of the British rule. Dr. Kwame Nkrumah announced Independence on March 6, 1957. I am blessed to be called more specifically, a Ghanaian-American.

Albion Mends III
Carolyn Ann Coffield

H is for hope.
My father is the oldest of nine children. He left Ghana, with the national track team, to train in America. He hoped to get a higher education and run in the Olympics. Dad met my African-American mother in college. They had so much hope for their family and made faith, love, and giving a priority in our daily lives.

Black History Month 1986 — The International Connection

International Club

I is for identity.
My identity was shaped by my parents' actions. Their engagement with family and community gave me the answers to my questions:
"Who am I?
Where did I come from?
Where do I belong?
How can I make a difference in the world?"

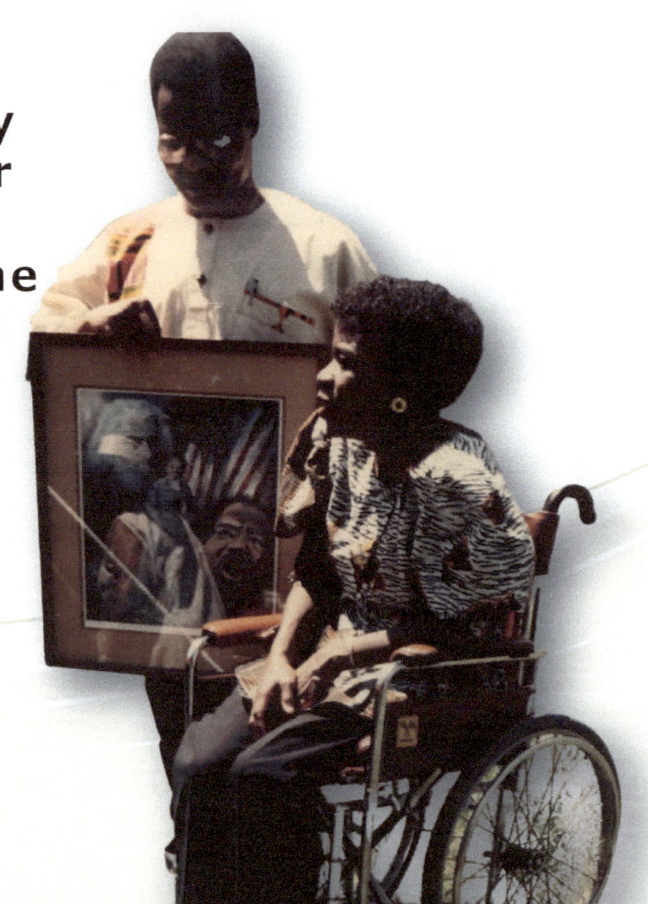

kente cloth

J is for joy. Tremendous joy filled my heart when my dad would visit my school. He played traditional instruments and taught classic games. We passed around cultural artifacts. The students asked questions about my name and how my family left Ghana. They asked my dad to describe life in his country.

K is for kind.
Children teased me and called me "Hakuna Matata." Their singing and laughing made me feel like I did not fit in. I felt lonely, embarrassed, and ashamed of my name. My parents talked to me and helped boost my confidence. They told me to be kind and remember our family values.

Have a good day, little love
Papa and Mama

Smiles, Tears, Solemn Faces

Trying to keep COOL

L is for legacy. In the evening, Mama and I would paint and craft pictures together. Adding fabric helped make the art look more authentically African. She showed me how to learn from my mistakes and be a creative teacher. Her art is a piece of a colorful legacy.

Fabric Folk Art
CAC

sandals with authentic kente cloth

M is for meals.
My name is also from a rich cooking culture. Foods are made to bring families together. Ghana is famous for fufu, jollof rice, fried plantains, meat stews, and spicy sauces. We make these dishes in America, but it is sometimes hard to find foods, spices, and tools to make the exact mouth-watering meals.

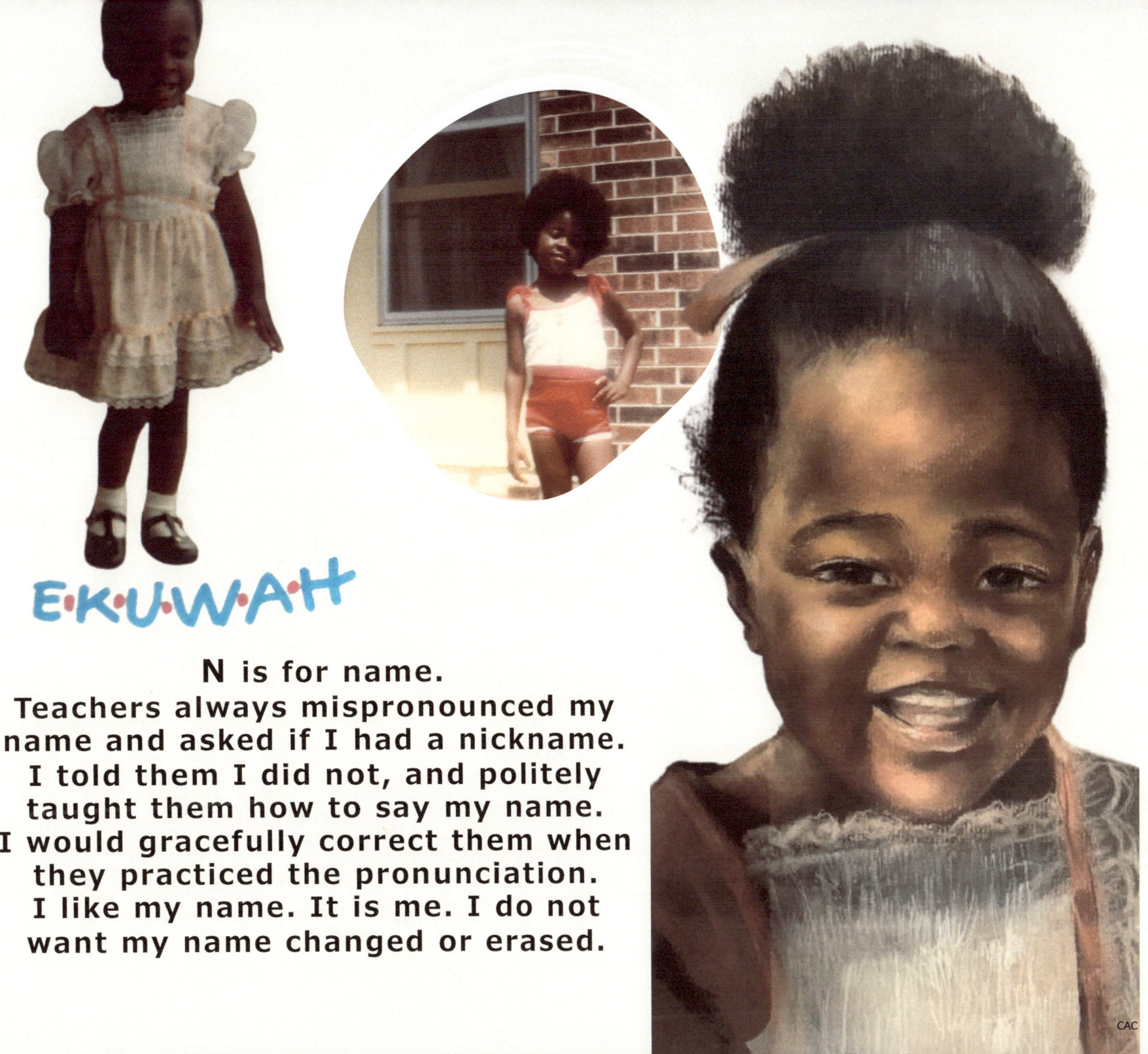

EKUWAH

N is for name.
Teachers always mispronounced my name and asked if I had a nickname. I told them I did not, and politely taught them how to say my name. I would gracefully correct them when they practiced the pronunciation. I like my name. It is me. I do not want my name changed or erased.

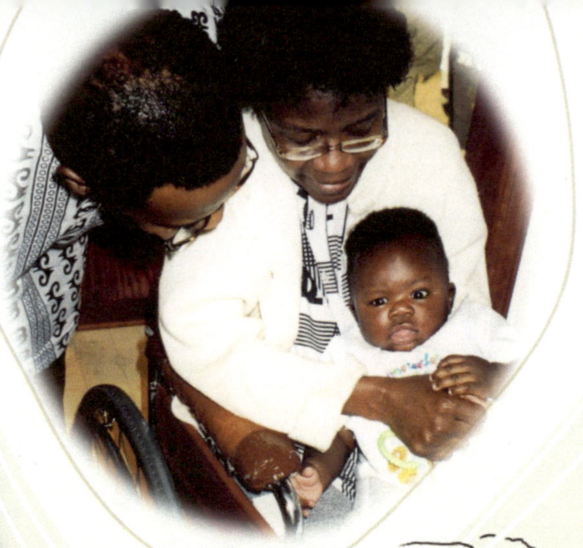

my son's outdooring

abofra
"BABY"

Outdooring

O is for observation.
A naming ceremony took place eight days after I was born. An "Outdooring" is a time for giving blessings and gifts for the baby. Family and friends were asked to dress in white. Dad wanted our Missouri friends to observe that culture starts at birth and travels with us.

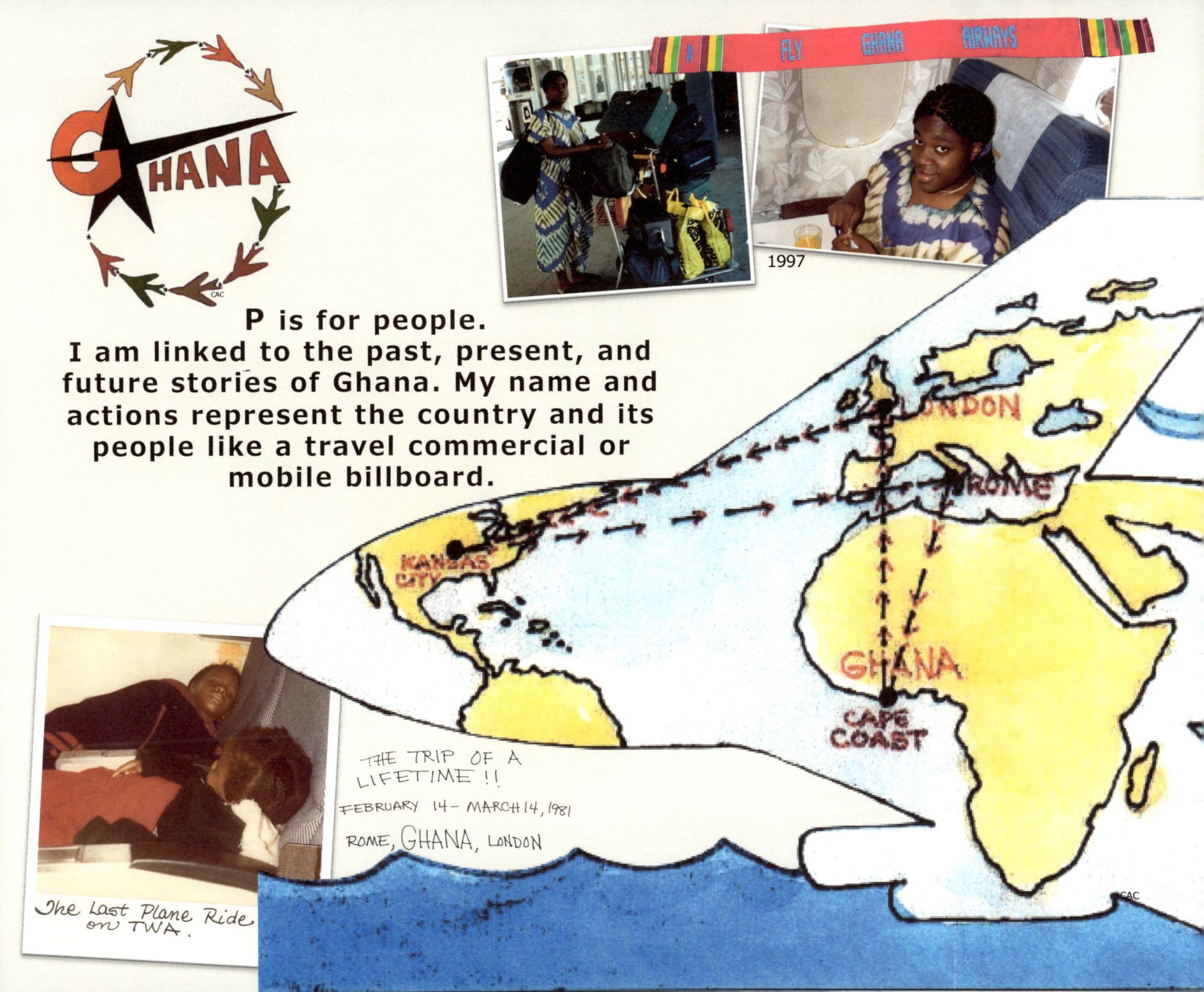

P is for people.
I am linked to the past, present, and future stories of Ghana. My name and actions represent the country and its people like a travel commercial or mobile billboard.

Q is for questions. My parents knew I would have a lot of questions. Mom created homemade books for me to learn about Ghana. The pages included the English and Fante language. We read those books together over and over. I still ask questions and try to learn more about our language, history, and culture each day.

Mema wo akye
"GOOD MORNING!"

MOBUUKUU A ODZIKAN
My First Book

BUILDING Baby Mends' EARLY YEARS

Mefie
My House

R is for roots.
My family placed a golden Sankofa bracelet in a time capsule. Mama buried it under a tree on my first birthday. It reminds us to keep growing where we are planted. My roots began long before the slave trade and colonization.

S is for symbol.
In Ghana, Sankofa means to "go back to fetch it." It is an Adinkra symbol of wisdom - learning from the past, in building for the future. The symbol is often printed on fabric, carved into wood, and more.

T is for treasure.
Mama and Papa taught us to value the art of Ghana. We have unique handmade artifacts from our visits. The decorations in my home point to an address just like my name does.

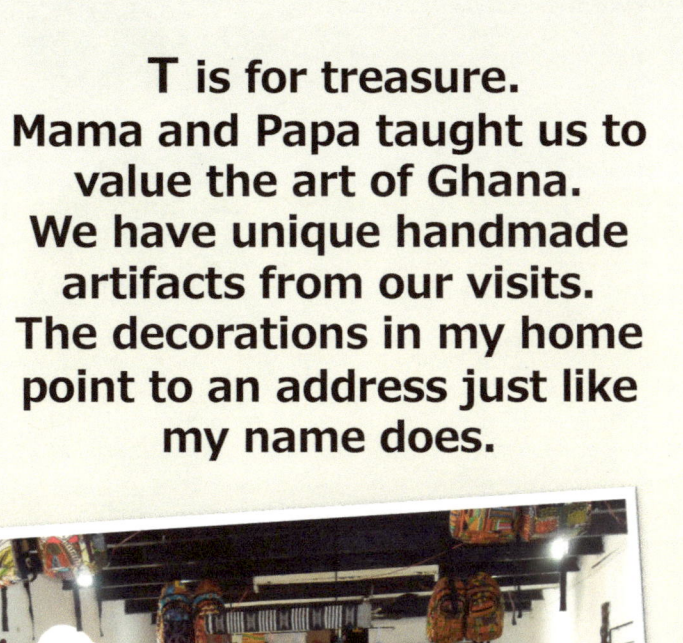

2013

Fabric Folk Art (CAC)

V is for variety.
There is peace between the many tribes in Ghana. Language, food, religion, and festivals vary by region. The Ashanti tribe spells and says my name differently - Akua.

Fabric Folk Art (CAC)

If **boy** — the name will be

SUNDAY	KWESI DAVID
MONDAY	KODWO DAVID
TUESDAY	KOBENA DAVID
WEDNESDAY	KWEKU DAVID
THURSDAY	DAVID ANAMOAH
FRIDAY	KOFI DAVID
SATURDAY	KWAME DAVID

David - Hebrew meaning "BELOVED ONE"

girl — the name will be

SUNDAY	EWURESI RUTH
MONDAY	ADWOWA RUTH
TUESDAY	ARABA RUTH
WEDNESDAY	EKUWAH RUTH
THURSDAY	ABA RUTH
FRIDAY	EFFUAH-RUTH
SATURDAY	AMA RUTH

Ruth - Hebrew meaning "FRIEND"

**W is for why.
Ekuwah identifies the day of the week I was born and my gender. I am a girl born on Wednesday. Babies born on Wednesday are the famous and fearless ones, ask Kweku Anansi the Spider!**

United We Stand, Divided We Fall
(made from one piece of wood)

Motivational Greeting Card
(based on the folktale of the eagle raised among chickens)

X is for x-factor.
The variable in Ghana is opportunity. Hard work and perseverance are expected. The village helps me to fly higher and higher. They remind me to get back up again when I struggle. The cultural belief is, "your success is our success."

Y is for yes.
As elders say at an outdooring, "Let your 'yes' be 'yes,' and your 'no' be 'no.'" I always strive to be honest. Life and a good family name are fragile. I choose to handle both with care.

egg carving representing life's fragility

Z is for zest.
Grandpa is 102 years old and lives life with zest. He likes to crack a witty joke, give a loving smile, or unexpectedly sing an inspirational tune. I am proud to represent him, my family, the country of Ghana, and the African ancestors who paved the way for me. My name is an address. What is your address?

1976

1998
(my wedding)

2015

Albion Mends II
2019

Pronunciation Guide

	Common Akan Pronunciation	Meaning
adinkra	ah-DINK-ra	farewell or goodbye
Akua	ay-KWEE-ah	Girl "Born on Wednesday"
Ashanti	ah-SHAN-tee	A major ethnic group living in Central Ghana
Ekuwah / Ekua	ay-KOO-ah	Girl "Born on Wednesday"
Fante	FAHN-tee	an Akan people
Kawanupadu	ka-WAH-nu-PAA-du	Shut your mouth
sankofa	san-KO-fah	Learn from the past to build the future

This is an unfinished painting from my mother's to-be-completed pile.

Visit my website for more pronunciations, videos, activities, and a discussion guide!

What's Your Ghanaian Name?

Most Ghanaian names are based on the day of a child's birth and their gender. Visit my website to enter your birthdate and gender. Then, read and hear your name in the most widely spoken language in Ghana.

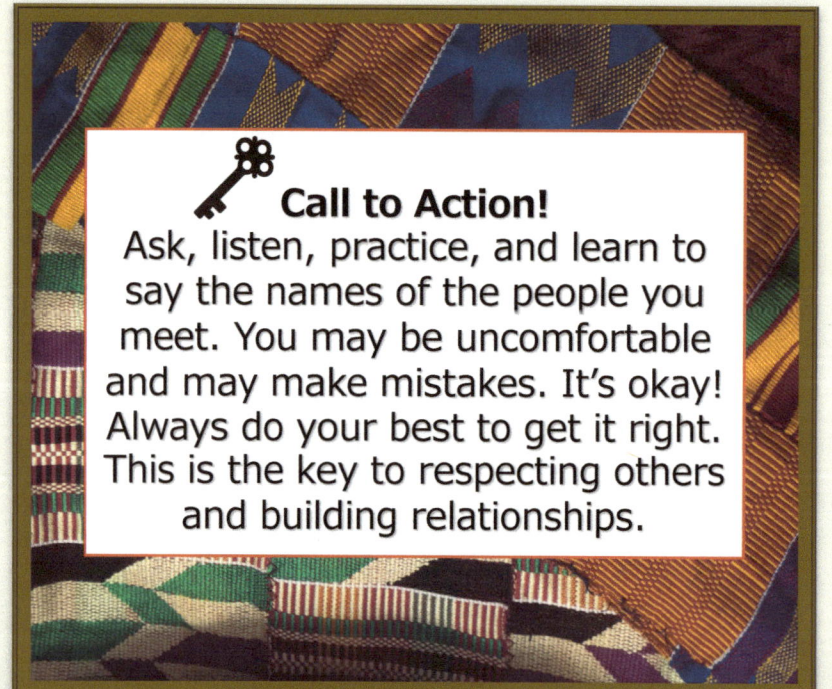

Call to Action!
Ask, listen, practice, and learn to say the names of the people you meet. You may be uncomfortable and may make mistakes. It's okay! Always do your best to get it right. This is the key to respecting others and building relationships.

Carolyn Coffield Mends (CAC)

(January 3, 1951 – July 13, 2017)

Carolyn Ann Coffield was born in Hobbs, New Mexico. On January 27, 1973, she and Albion Mends III were united in marriage in Portales, New Mexico. They moved to Warrensburg, Missouri in 1974. In 1975, she was diagnosed with Multiple Sclerosis (MS) and survived a breast cancer diagnosis in 1996. Mrs. Mends refused to let it define her life or impact her gift of giving and service.

Carolyn was also an accomplished and award-winning artist with work displayed, sold and distributed world-wide. She often stated her talent was a natural gift enlarged by academic study. She earned both her BA in art and a MA in secondary education from Eastern New Mexico University in Portales, New Mexico.

She was an impactful academic advisor at Central Missouri State University (now UCM) for 22 years. Carolyn worked with thousands of students in this role and as a student organization advisor or co-advisor with her husband. Serving the Association of Black Collegiates, Harambee, and Sisters of Ujima (an organization she founded and created), she also served on various committees and assisted with University initiatives. She received numerous accolades, awards, and honors for her work in student affairs and engagement.

Written by Effuah Sam

MoDOT ADOPT-A-HIGHWAY
Litter Cleanup
1.0 Miles

SISTERS OF UJIMA
FOUNDED BY
CAROLYN MENDS

About Ekuwah

Ekuwah [Mends] Moses has a BA in Elementary and Early Childhood Education from the University of Central Missouri. She has a MA in Teaching and Learning - Elementary Reading from Nova Southeastern University. She is a published International Literacy Association author learning alongside educators and families in Las Vegas, Nevada. This is her 20th year in education. She previously worked as a Performance Zone Instructional Coach, K-5 Literacy Specialist, Learning Strategist, and elementary classroom teacher. Ekuwah values quality time with her husband and two teenagers. This is her debut children's book. Ekuwah invites you to contact her via the website or social media.

#MyNameIsAnAddress

Website: ekuwah.com

Twitter: @Ekuwah

Instagram: @ekuwah_m

Facebook: Ekuwah Moses, Author

www.ingramcontent.com/pod-product-compliance
Lightning Source LLC
Chambersburg PA
CBHW041148070526
44579CB00004B/52